W0275135

REBEL GIRLS
5-MINUTE STORIES

This is a work of creative nonfiction. It is a collection of heartwarming and thought-provoking stories inspired by the lives and adventures of 10 influential women. It is not an encyclopedic account of the events and accomplishments of their lives.

www.rebelgirls.com
Rebel Girls, Inc.
421 Elm Ave.
Larkspur, CA 94939
Printed in China
UID: 001-351116-Sep/25
10 9 8 7 6 5 4 3 2 1

Lek Chailert, the Elephant Whisperer: text adapted from an audio story by Sara Weiss, illustrations by Nathalia Takeyama. *Ada Lovelace Cracks the Code*: text adapted from a chapter book by Corinne Purtill, illustrations by Marina Muun. *Dr. Wangari Maathai Plants a Forest*: text adapted from a chapter book by Corinne Purtill, illustrations by Eugenia Mello. *Alfonsina Strada and the Big Bike Race*: text adapted from a picture book by Elena Favilli, illustrations by Laura Proietti. *Autumn Peltier, the Water Protector*: text adapted from an audio story by Alexis Stratton, illustrations by Aly McKnight. *Simone Biles Tumbles to Triumph*: text adapted from an audio story by Farrah Penn, illustrations by Monica Mikai. *Alicia Alonso Takes the Stage*: text adapted from a chapter book by Nancy Ohlin, illustrations by Josefina Preumayr. *Taylor Swift Dreams in Lyrics*: text by Eliza Kirby and Jess Harriton, adapted from an audio story by Frances Thomas, illustrations by Paula Zorite. *Junko Tabei Masters the Mountains*: text adapted from a chapter book by Nancy Ohlin, illustrations by Montse Galbany. *Madam C.J. Walker Builds a Business*: text adapted from a chapter book by Denene Millner, illustrations by Salini Perera.

Art direction by Giulia Flamini
Cover illustrations by Nathalia Takeyama (Lek Chailert), Eugenia Mello (Wangari Maathai), Paula Zorite (Taylor Swift), Aly McKnight (Autumn Peltier), Laura Proietti (Alfonsina Strada), Monica Mikai (Simone Biles), Salini Perera (Madam C.J. Walker), Josefina Preumayr (Alicia Alonso)
Layout by Kristen Brittain and Giulia Flamini
Edited by Eliza Kirby and Sarah Parvis
Special thanks: Amy Pfister, Jess Harriton, Hannah Bennett, Michon Vanderpoel

A CIP catalogue record for this book is available from the British Library.
ISBN: 978-0-2417-5917-2

The authorised representative in the EEA is
Dorling Kindersley Verlag GmbH. Arnulfstr. 124,
80636 Munich, Germany

This book was made with Forest Stewardship Council™ certified paper – one small step in DK's commitment to a sustainable future. Learn more at **www.dk.com/uk/information/sustainability**

CONTENTS

When you come across a QR code in this book, scan it, and you'll be whisked away on an audio adventure.

LEK CHAILERT

THE ELEPHANT WHISPERER

Deep in the forests of northern Thailand, there lived a girl named Saengduean Chailert. Everyone called her Lek, a Thai word for "small one". Lek had an unusual best friend. His name was Thong Kham, and he was an elephant. Nothing brought Lek more joy than watching Thong Kham romp in the mud, his paper-thin ears flapping in the breeze. Lek felt like Thong Kham was part of her family.

Lek and Thong Kham loved exploring the wilderness together. Wherever they went, she brought his favourite snack – bananas. Thong Kham would grab the fruit with his trunk and toss it into his mouth, his tail swinging.

Then he would let out a low rumbling sound of appreciation as Lek petted his grey, leathery skin.

This was their special way of communicating. It was their way of saying to each other, *Thank you, I love you, and you're safe with me.*

When Lek was 16 years old, she saw something that changed her life. She was in the jungle when she heard elephants trumpeting in distress. When she found the elephants, they were straining hard, pulling heavy logs. They looked and sounded miserable.

Lek quickly learned that these were logging elephants. People used them to haul freshly cut trees. The elephants were often injured doing this work. Plus, the logging destroyed their natural habitats. The elephants were running out of safe places to live.

I have to do something to help them, Lek thought.

Over the next few years, Lek learned all she could about elephants. She soon understood how dire the situation was. Asian elephants had become endangered and could soon go extinct. They could disappear forever! She had to act now if she was going to save them.

So Lek started a mobile clinic called the Jumbo Express. She drove around to remote villages in a truck. In each place, she gave out medicine and soothed injured, neglected, or elderly elephants. She jostled along bumpy roads and winding mountain paths, spending all day in the sun or the mud. But the journey was always worth it.

Lek felt like she had a deep connection to these amazing animals. She spoke to them gently and listened to each of their rumbles and vibrations, just like she did with Thong Kham. Soon, she became known as the "elephant whisperer".

After travelling around with the Jumbo Express for a few years, Lek was able to buy a small plot of land and open a rescue mission. She began to gather sick and injured elephants, leading them back to her space to help them heal.

Then Lek received a very generous donation – 250 acres of land in the lush, mountainous Mae Taeng Valley of northern Thailand. She was so excited!

Lek and a trusted team of animal advocates got to work, clearing out the overgrown brush and planting banyan trees and acacia. Lek was determined to turn this stretch of land into an elephant sanctuary – a place where elephants could graze in the fields, bathe in the river, and live full, peaceful lives.

Elephant Nature Park became the first elephant sanctuary of its kind in Asia.

Lek made sure to welcome each elephant with love and respect as they adjusted to their new surroundings.

Many of the elephants were injured or orphaned. But with Lek's gentle care and medical attention, they were able to get better and form new herds. They splashed in the water, chewed on fresh leaves, and trumpeted with joy.

Lek and her team have rescued more than 200 elephants, as well as dogs, cats, goats, boars, rabbits, horses, wild birds, buffalo, and other animals. When any creature is brought to the park, it is greeted with soothing care and empathy.

In this special place, elephants don't have to haul heavy lumber. They can roam and heal, play, and make new friends. And they get all the bananas they'd like to eat.

Each day at Elephant Nature Park, Lek wanders down dirt paths, her long braid slung over one shoulder, mountains towering above her, a herd of elephants by her side.

The elephants pause to wrap their trunks around her like a hug. Though she is small in stature, Lek has made a massive impact on this planet. She truly leads with love in everything she does.

ADA LOVELACE

CRACKS THE CODE

Augusta Ada Byron lived in a big house just outside of London, England. It had a grand staircase, a huge hall, and a schoolroom for her lessons. Ada loved to learn. But she couldn't always focus on exactly what her governess was teaching her. How was she supposed to solve maths problems when there were so many questions and ideas bouncing around her brain?

Sometimes, Ada sang loudly from the top of the steps. Her voice made a wonderful rich sound as it echoed through the house. Other times, she pretended the kitchen was a witch's den full of bubbling cauldrons. She cackled as she danced about, upsetting her mother and getting in the cook's way. She got scolded a lot.

It wasn't that Ada wanted to be naughty. She wanted to please her mother and her governess. But she had so much energy that sitting still was simply impossible. Nobody seemed to understand Ada. She wanted someone she could play with and someone to tell her marvellous ideas – someone besides her cat! She had no one like that . . . yet.

One day, Ada got a new governess, Miss Stamp. She and Ada talked about all the ideas running through Ada's head. Unlike her other governesses, Miss Stamp listened to Ada. After so much loneliness, having a true friend living right in the house felt better than Ada could have possibly imagined.

Ada travelled all over Europe with Miss Stamp and her mother, learning as she went. She sailed on serene lakes, sketched glorious palaces, and visited exciting cities. In Italy, she saw something that fascinated her: the design for a flying machine. Nobody had built it yet, but it would allow a person to fly like a bird.

When Ada returned to England, she got straight to work. While her mother was away, she began to create a flying machine of her own in the barn. On her first try, with two ropes tied to her leather belt, she took a deep breath, ran a few steps forwards, lifted her feet off the ground, and—

Crash. She tumbled forwards out of the belt onto the floor.

What was she missing? *Of course – wings!*

She spent weeks designing a beautiful set of wings cut from silk. But when her mother returned, she was not impressed.

"What about your studies, Ada?" she asked angrily. She put a stop to Ada's fanciful inventing.

Ada got older, Miss Stamp moved away, and Ada left her imaginative experiments behind. But then she learned about an incredible invention being used in the real world. On a visit to a fabric factory with her mother, she saw a machine called a Jacquard loom.

On the older looms, weavers moved the threads by hand to make fabric. On a Jacquard loom, operators fed a long stretch of punch cards into the machine from the top. The holes in the cards told the machine what patterns to weave.

Ada was mesmerized.

At a party one night, Ada met a mathematician named Charles Babbage. She listened, riveted, as he talked about a machine he was working on. It could count numbers up to 10,000 and add and multiply large numbers – all without the mistakes that humans could make.

"But my next machine will be even better – the Analytical Engine!" Charles said. "It will be the size of a small train. I'll need several thousand cogwheels, and it will be controlled by a series of punch cards—"

"Just like a Jacquard loom!" Ada exclaimed.

"Yes," Charles said, "exactly."

Ada and Charles began puzzling through the challenges of the Analytical Engine together. It would be able to do any calculation – as long as it had a punch card to tell it what to do. The possibilities were endless!

But it was hard to convince the rest of the world that the Analytical Engine was valuable.

When someone wrote an article about the machine in French, Charles said, "Ada, you understand my machine better than almost anyone. I'd like you to translate the article. But I'd also like you to help people understand what this machine has the power to do."

Just as she had when she built her wings, Ada focused everything on her work.

She translated the article and wrote a set of notes to accompany it. Using simple language, she described how the machine could calculate answers. But it could do more than that, Ada explained. It might be able to work with complex maths problems, words, music notes, and maybe even pictures.

She wrote nonstop. In the end, Ada wasn't even named in the article, only listed as "the translator". Even if no one else ever knew all she had done to bring this work into the world, she would know.

Once the article was published, Ada thought offers of support for Charles's machine would flow in. But the letters never came. Sadly, some important people thought of Charles as a man who didn't finish the projects he started.

Ada was disappointed. But she kept her eye on the future, always looking for the next great invention.

One hundred years after her death, her fellow mathematicians rediscovered her work. They marvelled at how she had been able to predict so many of the possibilities computers held.

Ada and Charles never got to build the Analytical Engine. But with her imagination and perseverance, Ada helped open doors for inventors of the future. Today, Ada is considered one of the first computer programmers – before computers even existed.

WANGARI MAATHAI

PLANTS A FOREST

Wangari Maathai was born in a small village in central Kenya. She spent her childhood surrounded by spectacular trees like the giant mugumo tree, a tall, wild fig tree with bark as grey and gnarled as an elephant's hide. Nearby was a stream that bubbled up straight from the earth.

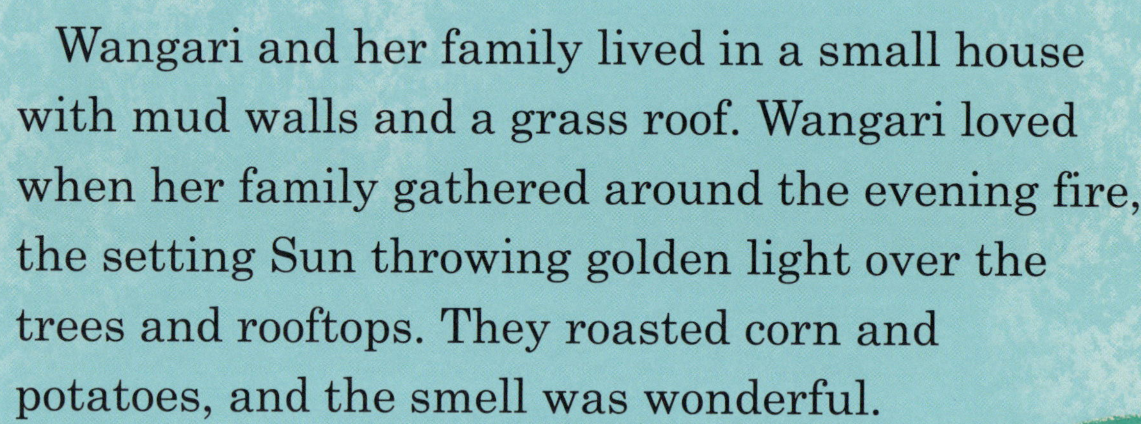

Wangari and her family lived in a small house with mud walls and a grass roof. Wangari loved when her family gathered around the evening fire, the setting Sun throwing golden light over the trees and rooftops. They roasted corn and potatoes, and the smell was wonderful.

"Tell us a story!" she and her siblings would call out to their mother.

"All right," their mother would say. She would pick up a knobbly tree root and begin shaving away the tough bark with her knife.

"One day, a long, long time ago," she would begin. And she would tell her children stories of the elephants, monkeys, and leopards that roamed the forests.

When Wangari's older brother Nderitu came home from boarding school, the two would run all over the village. They'd skip, jump, and play. They'd joke and slide down muddy hills in the rain.

Like many boys his age, Nderitu went to school. But, like many girls in her village, Wangari stayed home and helped with chores and taking care of the other children. She loved to read her brother's schoolbooks. And she soaked up knowledge like plants soaked up the sun.

One day, she came home from collecting firewood and found her house full of people. Her mother, her uncle, and her grandfather smiled at her. They had news: Wangari was going to school!

Wangari spent three years at her local primary school. Then she was ready for a new adventure. She packed up her books and her brand-new school uniform. She and brother started the four-hour walk to the nearby town of Nyeri. She'd never slept away from home before. She'd never even crossed a bridge before!

But Wangari knew that the rest of her life was just across that river. So she took a deep breath, kept her eyes straight ahead, and crossed to the other side.

Wangari was an excellent student. When she was 16, she earned a scholarship to a high school just outside of Nairobi, the capital of Kenya. And off she went!

Science came easily to Wangari. She loved biology, chemistry, and the magic and wonders of the natural world.

Wangari had a science teacher named Mother Teresia, who taught Wangari about biology and chemistry. They did experiments. And Wangari learned about the atoms, molecules, and cells that are the building blocks of life – from the smallest tadpole to the tallest tree.

When Mother Teresia asked Wangari what she wanted to do after high school, Wangari was stumped. She thought about what she was good at. She thought about the things she loved most. Then she made a plan. She would go to university!

After studying biology in the United States, Wangari returned to Kenya. When she stepped off the plane in Nairobi, the warm, dry air wrapped around her like a blanket. It was nothing like the snow she'd left behind!

Soon Wangari became the first female professor in East and Central Africa. She got married and had children. But she missed her village. It was time for a trip home.

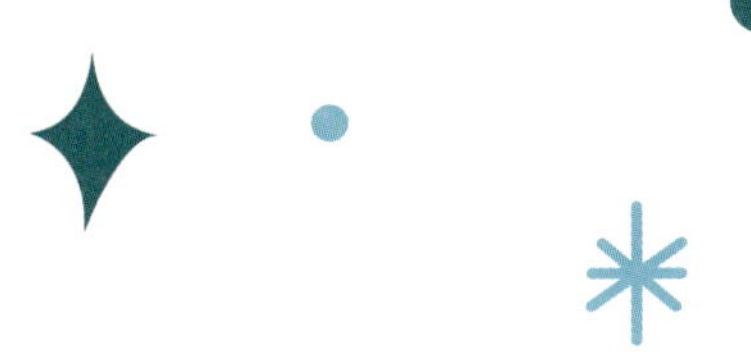

Back in her village, Wangari gave her mother the biggest hug ever. But she noticed that everything had changed. There were broad, dusty patches where groves of tall trees had once stood. The trees had been cut down to make room for coffee and tea plantations. The stream running along the road, which used to be clear and clean, was dirty.

They walked to where the kids used to slide in the mud. "Children can't play here during the rainy season anymore," her mother explained. "There have been too many landslides. And without the trees, we have to walk far away to find firewood and clean water."

Wangari thought about the problem. She knew that the women in her village needed firewood to cook. They needed food for their cattle and goats. They needed shade and fresh fruits – and healthy streams and soil to grow their crops. And what provides all that? Trees!

Wangari had an idea: the women of Kenya would plant trees and save their own land.

On June 5, 1977 – World Environment Day – Wangari threw a big party to show people just how easy it was to plant a tree.

In time, the trees they planted would be tall enough that their canopies would touch one another – like a green belt across the sky.

The Green Belt Movement! That is the perfect name for our project! thought Wangari. She travelled all over Kenya, finding more and more women to plant seedlings.

Some men didn't think women should be organizing or planting trees. Once a merchant refused to sell her seeds because he didn't believe women knew how to plant a forest. She showed him! He took one look at the thriving trunks, branches, and leaves of the trees Wangari's friends had planted and changed his mind.

Since they began, the women of the Green Belt Movement have planted more than 51 million trees. They also raise money so they can pay women to plant trees in their own communities. In this way, Wangari's movement helps the Earth *and* provides women and girls with meaningful work close to home.

Wangari knew that she and her friends were planting more than trees – they were planting ideas too.

In 2004, Wangari was awarded the Nobel Peace Prize. What did she do to celebrate? She dug a hole in the warm soil and planted another tree.

ALFONSINA STRADA

AND THE BIG BIKE RACE

When Alfonsina was growing up in Italy in the 1890s, most girls stayed home, cooking and sewing. Not Alfonsina! She was always outside, riding her papa's two-wheeled farming machine like a bike. Finally when she was 10, her papa gave in and bought her a bicycle of her own.

"Thank you, thank you, thank you!" Alfonsina exclaimed.

"Well, be careful—" her papa began.

But Alfonsina was already off. “Bye, Papa!” she called over her shoulder as she sped away. “I have many races to win!”

She spent the rest of the day zooming through town on her new bike. By the time the Sun set, her legs were sore from pedalling, but she’d never been so happy.

One day, Alfonsina heard about a famous bike race called the Giro d'Italia. The cyclists in the race rode for three weeks straight, covering 2,000 miles.

Alfonsina was excited.

"I want to race the Giro d'Italia!" she announced.

"Don't be silly," said her papa. "Women cannot race the Giro d'Italia. It's too tough."

"I'm tough!" Alfonsina replied.

Alfonsina trained hard, pedalling uphill and coasting downhill for hours a day. She signed up for races against girls *and* boys – and won. Even though her rickety bike was heavy and had only one speed, Alfonsina blew past all her competitors. Someday she'd be ready for the Giro d'Italia.

When Alfonsina got older, her papa said, "Enough with this bike! Women have to get married and take care of children."

That didn't sound right to Alfonsina. Why should she have to give up cycling?

She met a man named Luigi Strada. They fell in love and decided to get married – but Alfonsina didn't stop biking. Luigi even gave her a racing bicycle on their wedding day!

With her new bike, Alfonsina set a world speed record, riding 23 miles in just one hour. People called her the Devil in a Dress, and she became known as one of the best cyclists in Italy. When she travelled to Paris to race, Luigi cheered her on from the sidelines.

At last, Alfonsina was ready to race in the Giro d'Italia. A woman had never competed in it before, so she signed up using a man's name: Alfonsin Strada.

On the first day of the race, thousands of people lined the streets of Milan to watch. They whooped and hollered as the cyclists geared up for their long journey. Alfonsina felt nerves bubbling inside her at the starting line, but she was determined as she mounted her bike. And then – they were off!

For two weeks, Alfonsina pedalled hard, fueled by the crowds' *oohs* and *aahs* along the way. Their eyes widened in surprise as she passed – *Was that a woman speeding by?* But by the time they tried to get a second look, Alfonsina had left them in the dust.

The race was going smoothly until all of a sudden . . .

RAIN! Heavy rain! Alfonsina's wheels slipped in the mud, and she fell. Once she got back up, she toppled again, this time breaking her handlebars.

Alfonsina held the ruined pieces in her hands. "What am I going to do?" she groaned.

A farmer watching from the side of the road could see she was in trouble. "I have an old broomstick . . . Would that help?" he asked.

Aha! Alfonsina took the broomstick and made a quick repair. She hopped back on her bike, muscles screaming as she pedalled as fast as she could. By now, she was way behind the other riders, bruised and exhausted. But the crowds urged her to keep going.

Alfonsina raced through twists and turns, mountain passes, and riverbanks. She zipped through cities and towns.

Everyone was amazed by – and curious about – this new cyclist. *Could that racer really be a woman?* One day in the middle of the race, the front-page story in the newspaper read: "Alfonsina and the Bike: One Woman Among Men." The crowds couldn't get enough of her.

At last, Alfonsina approached the end of the race. Throngs of people were waiting for her there, hooting and shouting.

When Alfonsina crossed the finish line in Milan, tears of pride and relief tumbled down her cheeks. The cheering spectators welcomed her back. She was sore and weary from the weeks of racing, falling, and getting back up again to race some more. But she had made it!

Alfonsina was the first and only woman to ever race the Giro d'Italia. She always knew that cycling was her path, and she trained to be the best.

Alfonsina didn't let people tell her that girls shouldn't or couldn't do something. Instead, she biked as fast as she could and surrounded herself with people who believed in her dreams and supported her as an athlete.

She became a hero in Italy and throughout the world.

AUTUMN PELTIER

THE WATER PROTECTOR

From the time she was small, Autumn loved to celebrate the beauty of rivers, lakes, and oceans. She learned from her Elders in the Wiikwemkoong First Nation how to perform water ceremonies.

During these special gatherings, Autumn would dip a special copper cup into the surface of a lake or river. Then she would lift the water up high and sing prayers of protection.

One day, when Autumn was eight, her mum and great-aunt Josephine brought her to a water ceremony in Ontario. Autumn felt strong as she looked out across the glittering Snake River. Everything was going as usual until she took a break to go to the bathroom.

Signs seemed to shout at her from the walls: Don't drink the water!

Autumn's eyes widened.

"Why can't we drink the water?" Autumn asked her mum.

"It isn't clean," her mum said. "The water has pollution from landfills, oil spills, and old mines."

Autumn was confused. How could people do this to the water? And to Mother Earth?

Autumn learned that many First Nations communities in Canada had been living with polluted water for many, many years. They had to use bottled water for drinking, cooking, and taking baths. Some had to boil their water to make it safe to use.

Autumn was outraged. But what could she do about this problem? She was just a kid.

She looked to her mum and great-aunt Josephine for guidance. Years ago, Josephine had walked all the way around Kitchi-Gami, also known as Lake Superior. It took her more than a month. As she walked, she prayed for the healing of the lake. She spoke to people about how pollution was making the water sick.

Her journey inspired a whole movement of water walkers, who walked and prayed for the water in their communities. And it inspired Autumn.

With her mum and great-aunt Josephine's encouragement, Autumn started speaking out at her school and in her community. Standing tall in front of her class, her voice carried across the room. Did her classmates know that some kids their age couldn't just turn on the tap and fill a cup with water?

"Water hears, feels, and listens to us," she said. "But it can't speak words the same way we do. People like me have to speak for the water."

If everyone worked together, she explained, they could help the water heal.

Autumn's Elders were so impressed that a few years later, they invited her to an important meeting. The prime minister of Canada would be there!

Autumn spent three days preparing a speech, writing every word by hand. Her mum made her a special dress. It was a deep navy blue with bright flowers and birds sewn into the fabric.

But when she got there, the organizers told Autumn not to say anything to the prime minister. They told her to walk up, present him with a gift, and leave. Autumn shook her head. She couldn't be silent! This was her one opportunity to do something – something big.

She walked towards the prime minister, and he looked down at her with a soft smile.

Autumn knew this was her cue to hand over the gift and walk away. But instead, she stopped. She summoned all the courage she had from her mum, her great-aunt, and from the water itself.

"I'm very unhappy with the choices you've made and your broken promises to my people," Autumn said, her voice shaking but sure.

The prime minister looked a little shocked, but he nodded. "I understand that."

Tears welled in Autumn's eyes. She held out her gift: a ceremonial water bowl, just like the ones she used when she sang the special words of protection over lakes, rivers, and oceans. It was copper with a red cloth and shiny cup inside.

"I will protect the water," the prime minister promised. He took the bowl in his hands. Autumn hoped he felt its power and responsibility.

Two years later, Autumn was invited to speak in front of the United Nations. This was her chance to share her message with a group of leaders from all over the world.

Autumn's mother booked them a flight from Toronto to New York City.

But it was cancelled three times.

So they loaded up their car and drove for 15 hours. As the New York City skyline grew bigger on the horizon, Autumn and her mum breathed sighs of relief.

They had made it!

At the United Nations meeting, a big crowd of leaders gathered to hear Autumn's speech.

As Autumn approached the microphone, butterflies flitted in her stomach. She stepped carefully up to the podium and took a long, deep breath. "I am lending my voice to speak up for water, and Mother Earth. We cannot just pray anymore," said Autumn. "We must do something, and we must do it now."

When she finished her speech, the room erupted with applause.

Autumn's work is not always easy. In the difficult moments, she remembers all the people who came before her. She closes her eyes and imagines she's walking with her great-aunt Josephine, circling the great lake Kitchi-Gami.

The lake's waters lap at the shore and a cool breeze blows ripples across the surface. With each step, Autumn feels the calm strength of her Ancestors. She feels the power of the water leading her forwards.

SiMONE BiLES

TUMBLES TO TRiUMPH

Six-year-old Simone stepped into the gym, eyes wide with wonder. She ignored the smell of chalk dust and feet and watched girls doing cartwheels and flips. *I can do that*, she thought. She stepped onto a mat and did a backflip.

A coach spotted her and asked, "How long have you been doing gymnastics?"

"I've never taken a lesson," Simone replied.

After her first visit to the gym, Simone's parents signed her up for classes. One day, she was practising flipping on the uneven bars when her hand slipped and she fell, landing on the floor with a loud *smack*.

She felt tears in her eyes.

Her coach called, "Try again!"

"No!" Simone cried. Falling from the bars had felt so scary. What if she fell again?

"You can do it," her coach told her. "Great gymnasts get back up." She helped Simone onto the bars again, guiding her through the motion of the flip.

Simone realized what her coach was trying to show her: even though she was scared, she could always try again.

Over the years, Simone continued to train and challenge herself. Her goal was to make it to the Olympics.

With her new trainer, Coach Aimee, Simone practised and practised.

She swung around and around the uneven bars. She launched herself over the vault. And she sailed from corner to corner of the floor exercise mat, springing a little higher and flipping a little faster each time.

Simone's training made her stronger in her mind and her body. She learned to trust herself, especially when it came to trying new moves. To make the Olympic team, Simone had to perfect a complicated vault called an Amanar. With a running start, she'd have to fly into a back handspring and then do two and a half twists high above the mats on the floor.

Simone stood at the end of the runway to the vault. Her mind filled with worries: *What if I can't do it? What if I get hurt?* But she knew she needed to master it.

Taking a deep breath, Simone sprinted down the runway. She leaped onto the springboard. Her hands met the surface of the vault, and she twisted through the air. Then her feet hit the ground. She stumbled backwards.

But she didn't fall over.

Coach Aimee was already walking over to tell her what else she could improve on. Simone knew her vault wasn't perfect. She'd taken a few steps on the landing, but she'd done it!

When the national team was announced, Simone's name was on the list! She couldn't believe it. At her first-ever Olympic Games, all of Simone's training paid off. She won four gold medals and one bronze, skyrocketing to the top of her sport.

Simone wowed crowds with the difficulty of her stunts. She even invented her own flips and twists.

At the US Championships, she stood on the balance beam in a sparkly silver-and-green leotard. She was nervous, but as always, she listened to her body. She pointed her foot out in front of her and paused before throwing herself into the back handsprings that would help her pick up speed.

Then she soared off the beam, completing a double-twisting double somersault before landing on the mat.

With her arms held high above her head and a smile on her face, she radiated confidence and joy.

In that moment, Simone became the first person to land a double-double dismount on the balance beam. That move is now known as the Biles.

And that is just one of the amazing moves named after her. In the Biles II, Simone runs across the mat and then launches herself into the air, where she does two backflips while twisting three times. She's like a spinning top – with wings!

Simone knew to trust her body. It would tell her when she needed to run a bit faster, tuck her body in a bit tighter, or rotate a bit more. And she knew to trust her body when it told her she needed a break.

At her second Olympics, Simone was buzzing with excitement as the event began. But during the vault competition, something went wrong. In the middle of her vault, Simone lost track of where she was. *Which way is up?* she thought, terrified, as she spun through the air. She landed on her feet, but just barely.

Simone was shaken. She didn't want to let down her team. She didn't want to disappoint her coach. She had always gotten up and tried again, but this time felt different. This time felt dangerous. Simone made the decision to pull out of her next event.

Simone stayed on the sidelines, proudly cheering on her team. After a few days, she felt ready to come back for her final event on the balance beam. She scaled back her routine, making sure she stayed safe – and won the bronze medal.

Simone showed the world a different kind of bravery – the courage to step back when something didn't feel right, the courage to take care your herself.

And then she showed the world that she could get back up. After the Olympics, she kept training, competing, and breaking records.

Whatever's in store for her next, Simone is ready to face it with courage and determination. There's a reason she's known as the greatest of all time!

ALICIA ALONSO

TAKES THE STAGE

Each night in their living room in Havana, Cuba, Alicia's family put on a talent show. A warm breeze carried the smell of saltwater through the open windows as everyone prepared their act. Her mother recited poetry, her brothers sang, and her sister hummed. Alicia always danced.

When the family moved to Spain for a year, Alicia took Spanish dance lessons. She caught on right away, her arms and legs moving gracefully to the music. From the record player, the clacking sound of castanets joined the other instruments.

Alicia loved the castanets' fierce, confident rhythm. It made her body feel fierce and confident too.

As their time in Spain came to an end, Alicia knew she wanted to keep dancing.

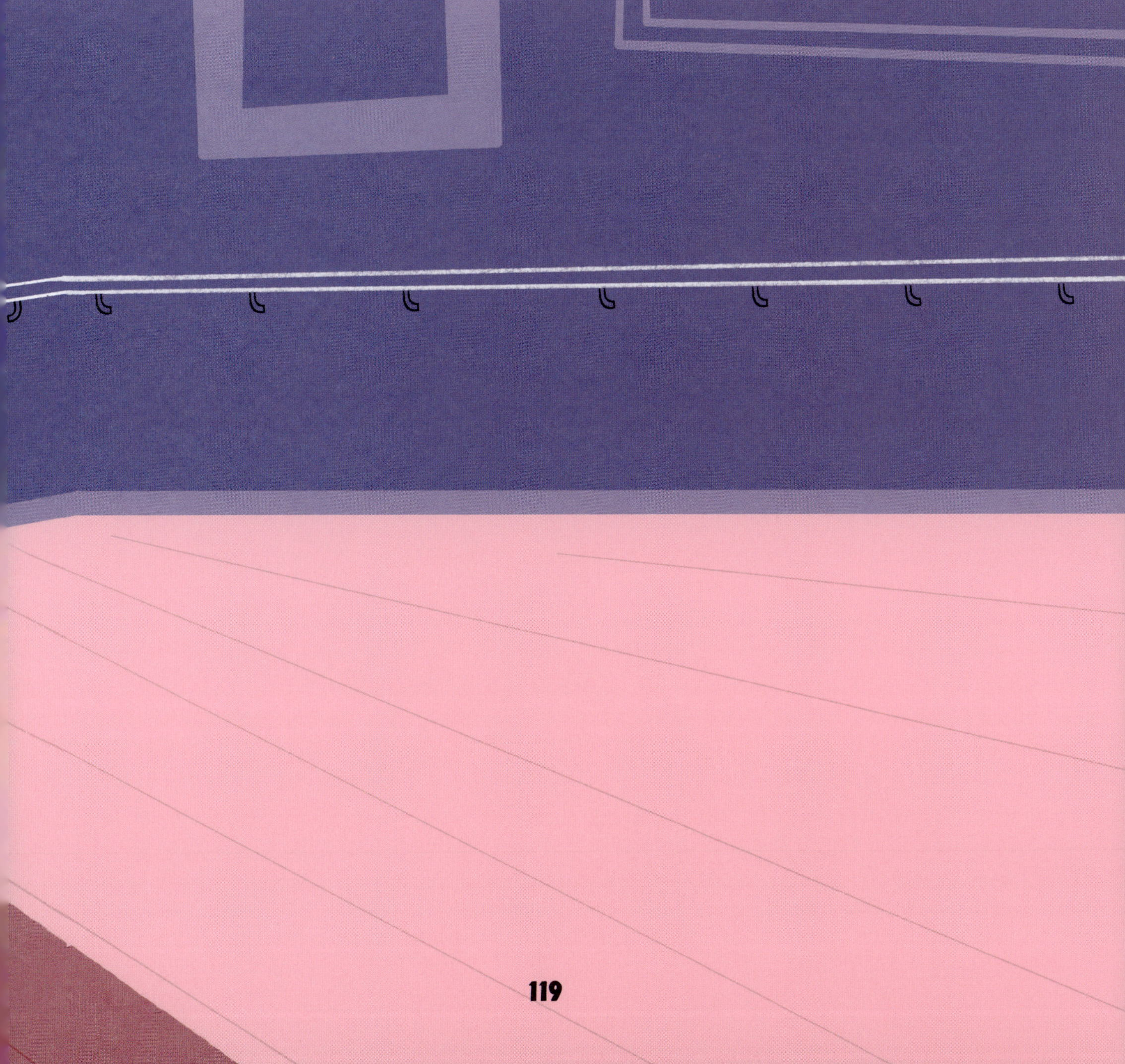

Back in Cuba, her mother could find lessons for only one style of dance: ballet. It was totally new for Alicia, but she was hooked right away. She loved telling stories and expressing emotions through graceful movements.

In one ballet, *Coppélia*, she danced a duet with a boy named Alberto. Their feet flew through the complicated steps, and Alberto lifted Alicia so high it felt like she could touch the stage lights. After they took their bows, someone threw a bouquet onto the stage. Alicia clasped it to her chest, beaming.

After the show, Alicia met Alberto's brother, Fernando. Fernando was impressed by Alicia's talent, and before long she convinced him to take ballet classes too.

Fernando and Alicia began dancing together all the time. Soon they fell in love. They thought a lot about their future. They had learned so much in Havana, but there were other cities with bigger, better stages for them.

So they got married and moved far from home, into a cramped apartment in New York City.

Alicia and Fernando got jobs in musical theater. But Alicia dreamed of becoming a professional ballerina.

At last, she landed a spot at a major ballet company. She earned many roles because she was so talented at expressing her emotions onstage.

Alicia felt unstoppable.

One day in rehearsal, Alicia heard a shout behind her: “Look out!”

It was too late. She bumped into a tall set piece and stumbled backwards. A fellow dancer caught her before she fell. The rest of the company gathered around her, concerned.

“Are you all right? Should we take a break?” the stage manager asked.

“I’m fine,” Alicia said, dazed. “We need to keep rehearsing.”

But just a few moments later, she collided with another dancer. Alicia blinked. She hadn’t seen him there at all. What was going on?

Alicia went home to rest, her mind full of worries. She had begun seeing little black spots in her vision, and over the past few days, they had gotten worse.

Her doctor told her she needed an operation on her eyes. But the recovery would be difficult. She would need to stay in bed, completely motionless, for an entire year.

Alicia knew she had no choice. She had the operation and went back to Cuba, where she could rest surrounded by her whole family.

Alicia stayed as still as she could. Even so, her doctor warned, she had lost a lot of her vision. She might never dance again.

Her chest tightened with anguish. She wanted to cry, but she wasn't allowed to do even that. What could she do?

Lying in bed, Alicia found a way to dance.

She danced in her head. She also danced with her fingers on top of her blankets, which she imagined as a stage.

Sometimes, Fernando would observe and correct her “choreography.” Humming along to the ballet *Giselle*, Alicia took her fingers through arabesques and jetés.

When the year was up, Alicia expected her vision to be much better. But it was almost as bad as it was before. Even walking was hard after so long in bed.

Slowly, Alicia's eyesight improved a little, and she got steadier on her feet. She began to go on walks with her dog, venturing farther each day. And eventually, she took up ballet again, first in Havana, then in New York.

A month after she returned to New York, the choreographer pulled Alicia aside. "Markova is sick. Do you think you can dance Giselle in her place?"

Alicia couldn't believe it. Delighted, she practically yelled, "I'd love to!"

"Good. We only have five days before the performance," the choreographer said.

Only five days?

Alicia thought back to her fingertip performances across her bedspread, the music to *Giselle* echoing through her mind. *You can do it, Alicia,* she told herself. She'd overcome bigger obstacles before. She started rehearsing right away.

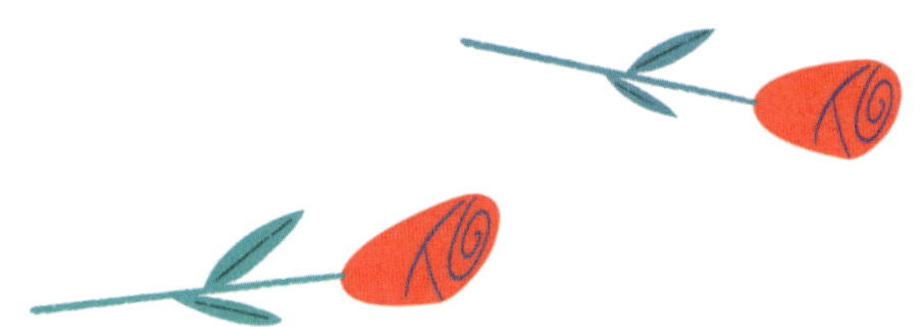

When the night of the performance arrived, Alicia stepped onstage as the music swelled. Under the lights, she became Giselle, just as she had in Havana while lying in bed with her eyes covered in bandages.

After the finale, the audience burst into applause. They threw bouquets on the stage and shouted "Brava!" over and over again.

Alicia gazed out at the crowd, who were on their feet now. They looked like fuzzy, blurry shadows to her, but she didn't care. She'd made it.

She truly was unstoppable.

TAYLOR SWIFT

DREAMS IN LYRICS

Every year around the holidays, the sprawling Christmas tree farm where Taylor grew up transformed into a bustling winter wonderland draped in lush green holly and mistletoe. Taylor loved to stroll through the snow-capped pines and race down slick hills on her sled.

One day, while rummaging through her parents' music collection, six-year-old Taylor found an album with a woman on the cover who looked just like her. Taylor put on the album and instantly fell in love with LeAnn Rimes's soaring vocals and dreamy lyrics.

Each song felt like a fabulous story, full of love and longing. Taylor dreamed of being a country singer like LeAnn, belting out lyrics in arenas around the world.

Taylor learned her favourite country music stars got their start in Nashville, Tennessee. So she begged her mum to take her there. In Nashville, Taylor went to Music Row, a street lined with record labels and recording studios. She knocked on every door, handing tapes of her singing to whoever answered.

"Hello, My name is Taylor Swift and I—"

"Hello, my name is Taylor—"

"Hello, my name—"

No one was interested, but Taylor refused to give up. When she got home, she signed up to sing at karaoke contests and county fairs.

She told local sports teams she was available as an opening act. Soon enough, she was singing at every baseball diamond and basketball court in town.

But as her singing career picked up, things at school began to slide downhill. Taylor got teased about her wild, curly hair, about being tall and gangly, and even about singing country music.

Instead of letting all those mean words intimidate her, Taylor used her feelings to inspire her music. She started writing her own lyrics, turning tough moments into catchy hooks and verses.

When Taylor was 13, her parents moved the family to Nashville. By now, she had a new tape full of original songs. She marched back to Music Row.

"Hello, my name is Taylor Swift, and I've got something you need to hear."

This time, Taylor got a recording contract, and her career exploded. She took the stage with fierce confidence, trained her voice to reach every corner of the room, and even added in some dance moves.

When she was 16 years old, Taylor released her debut album. It was about her first year in high school. Her songs sprang to life, telling vivid tales of friendships, crushes, and heartache. The album shot to the top of pop and country charts.

And Taylor was just getting started.

Taylor poured herself into every song she wrote. Each album she created was like a different chapter, or era, of her life.

As a teenager, she strummed a bedazzled guitar and sang country songs about falling in love as she spun around the stage in a sparkly dress.

Later, she wrote catchy pop tunes that got people to dance.

Then she created powerful anthems about standing up for herself and never giving up.

As the years went on, Taylor recorded more music, won lots of awards, and kept topping the charts. Her lyrics made fans feel like she was speaking directly to them. They showed up by the thousands at her concerts, singing along to every word.

Being in the spotlight wasn't always easy. Just like when she was a kid, Taylor had to deal with bullies commenting on what she wore, what she said, and who she spent time with. But now, everywhere she went, there were cameras!

Anger and frustration. Jealousy and joy. Courage, silliness, and wonder – Taylor felt all the emotions. And she took her feelings and made them into melodies. She turned passion into poetry and sadness into songs.

She turned loneliness and love into lullabies and transformed heartaches, hope, and happiness into hits.

And so the little one with the wild curls and the big imagination grew up to be a superstar. But she'll always be the girl who likes to sled down hills on snowy days, wear sparkly clothes, and curl up with her cats as she writes pages of lyrics straight from her heart.

Whenever Taylor sings and dances onstage, she can hear the audience shouting the words along with her. Their voices lift her up. She beams with joy, happy that she never gave up on her dream.

JUNKO TABEI

MASTERS THE MOUNTAINS

When Junko's fourth-grade teacher asked who was interested in a field trip to the mountains, Junko volunteered right away. A second later, she doubted herself. She was no good at gym class or sports. What made her think she could climb a mountain?

But she decided to give it a try.

As the hiking trip wore on, Junko began to doubt herself again, even as she heard her classmates' encouraging calls.

"Come on, Jun-chan!"

"You've got this!"

Junko stopped in the middle of the steep, rocky trail, gasping for breath. She bent down and grabbed her knees, and her sun hat fell to the ground. Her teacher handed her a canteen of water.

"Keep drinking. Stay hydrated. And do your best!" he said.

Junko took a long swig of cool water. Then she kept going until she reached the top.

I did it! she thought. *I climbed a mountain!*

As Junko got older, she longed to keep climbing, but she had to focus on her studies. Soon it was time for a different adventure: college! At that time in Japan, it was still unusual for girls to go away to school. But Junko made the brave choice to go to a university in Tokyo, far from her family's small village.

In Tokyo, Junko felt out of place. College seemed like a private club where everyone knew how to act except for her. The students were so stylish and sophisticated. Junko's Japanese, with its rural accent, sounded different. And then there were the classes, which were difficult.

But one day, some students invited her on a hike.

The trip reminded Junko how much she loved climbing mountains. She loved the exhilaration and achievement she felt when she reached the top. She began planning trips for herself to the mountains around Tokyo. *I wonder if there's a climbing group I could join?* she thought.

Junko looked and looked, but it wasn't easy to find a club that would accept her. Most of them said NO WOMEN ALLOWED in their ads in big, bold letters.

Finally, she found one. With the Ryoho climbing club, Junko learned to scale steep rock faces using long stretches of rope.

Rock climbing could be dangerous, and everyone needed to rely on their fellow climbers to stay safe.

On one climbing trip, Junko found herself scaling a mountain behind Masanobu Tabei, a skilled and famous climber. They started chatting and soon were making plans to climb together.

Before long, they fell in love and got married. On their honeymoon, Masanobu said, "I don't want you to be some sort of traditional Japanese housewife. I want you to keep climbing higher and higher mountains, and I want to help you do that."

Junko knew she had found the perfect partner for her.

Masanobu kept his promise, and Junko kept climbing higher. She formed an all-female climbing group. Together, her club came up with a spectacular plan.

"The Ladies Climbing Club is planning to climb Mount Everest," Junko told Masanobu.

"That's incredible!" Masanobu cried. "You'll be the

first women ever to ascend the highest mountain in the world!"

There was so much to do to prepare. Training would take a year, and the trip would cost a lot of money. And the dangerous expedition would last months. Junko got down to planning. Then she and her club took off.

By May 4, 1975, Junko and her group had been on Mount Everest for a month and a half. TV crews sometimes followed them – the first all-female expedition on Everest was big news! Now, they were only a week away from the summit.

Just seven more days, and we'll achieve our goal, Junko thought as they pitched their tents for the night.

Cold but exhausted, Junko fell asleep at once. But then she awoke to a strange vibration. Before she knew what was happening, there was a deafening noise – *wham!* It was an avalanche.

The avalanche trapped the women beneath layers of snow and ice, but eventually, they were able to get free. It was a miracle everyone survived. Junko and the others spent several days recovering in their tents. They all wanted to continue up to the summit.

The team doctor tried to talk Junko into quitting. "You're not in any shape to climb. You need to rest."

"I'll be good to go in two days. I'm not quitting," she said.

Over the next week, more team members gave up because of their injuries, sickness, or fatigue. Finally, only Junko and one other climber remained.

On May 16, 1975, 12 days after the avalanche, Junko reached the summit.

"I made it!" she announced to the rest of the team on her walkie-talkie. She heard cheers and clapping and everyone shouting, "Congratulations!"

She had done it!

Junko couldn't climb any higher than Everest, but she kept climbing for the rest of her life.

MADAM C. J. WALKER

BUILDS A BUSINESS

Sarah's mama parted her hair into three sections: one in the front, two in the back. Sarah wiggled around, smiling. She loved feeling her mama's fingers in her hair.

The littlest of five siblings, Sarah was the first member of her family who hadn't been born into slavery. Now she would be the first to go to school.

Right away, Sarah loved her class. She loved how the chalk slid across the board. She loved learning how to form letters and numbers in wobbly lines at first and then in careful swirls.

But after only three months, the state of Louisiana decided not to spend money on school for Black children like Sarah. She had to go back to working in the fields and taking care of her family's home.

When Sarah grew up, she had a daughter of her own named Lelia. Sarah's time in the classroom had been short, but it made her realize how important learning was. When the time came, Sarah sent Lelia to school, doing her hair for the first day just like her own mother had done.

Eventually, Lelia graduated from high school and went to college. Sarah was proud. She also had more time to herself now. She went back to school, learning reading, maths, geography, and more. On the weekends, she helped a group raise funds for people who didn't have enough money.

Through it all, Sarah had trouble with her hair. It was rough and short, with flaky bald spots. No matter how hard she tried, she could not get her hair to grow.

One day, a woman named Annie Turnbo came to Sarah's door. She was selling a product she swore would help Sarah's hair grow.

Sarah wasn't sure.

"Why don't you come to my workshop?" Annie suggested. "In the meantime, let me wash your hair with my special shampoo."

When Annie finished washing, drying, and combing Sarah's hair, it felt soft and fluffy instead of wiry and tangled.

Sarah was convinced! After she went to Annie's workshop, she began selling the hair product to women all over the city.

It wasn't long before Sarah was outselling all the other saleswomen. But she began to wonder if she could go into business for herself. She had already thought of ways to make a product even better than Annie's.

She moved to Denver, Colorado, so she could start fresh in a new city. Then she gathered ingredients and got to work.

“Coconut oil and beeswax for softness. Geranium and violet for smell,” Sara whispered, changing the measurements from one tablespoon to two. She added ingredients, then took them away. She scribbled notes, then crossed them out. For months, she kept at it, until she had the perfect creaminess and smell. She called her new product Sarah’s Wonderful Hair Grower.

Sarah was bursting with excitement. But Sarah's Wonderful Hair Grower wasn't selling as well as she'd hoped.

It needs a better name, she thought.

At last, she had it: Madam C.J. Walker's Wonderful Hair Grower. *Madam* sounded important and high-quality, just like her product. And *C.J. Walker* sounded elegant.

As Madam C.J. Walker, she went to churches, community centres, and any place where Black women gathered. The new name did the trick. There were so many orders that Sarah could barely fill them. Luckily, Lelia had just finished beauty school and was ready to help her mum out, doing hair at Madam C.J. Walker's salon.

HAIR TONIC
HAIR TONIC
WALKER'S
GLOSSINE
HAIR PRESSING OIL

Soon, word of Sarah's success got back to Annie. Annie believed Sarah had stolen her recipe and slapped on a new label. She took out an advert in the newspaper. "Beware of copycats," Annie warned. "Madam C.J. Walker would have been bald-headed if it weren't for my help!"

Sarah snorted in disgust. "Annie Turnbo is wrong. She helped me get my start, but that's all." She took out her own advert, firing back at Annie.

So Annie announced that one of *her* stylists would be setting up shop in Sarah's city.

"Mama, what are we going to do?" Lelia asked. "I'm good, but another shop could really hurt our business."

"I'm not worried, and you shouldn't be either." Sarah tossed the newspaper into the trash. "I have a plan."

WALKER'S
GLOSSINE
HAIR
PRESSING
OIL
WALKER'S
GLOSSINE
HAIR
PRESSING
OIL
WALKER'S
GLOSSINE
HAIR
TONIC
HAIR

Sarah and Lelia hit the road. Everywhere they went, Sarah taught women how to use the Walker Method. She also encouraged them to open up their own shops, selling her products. She had become a successful businesswoman, and they could too!

Unfortunately for Annie, Sarah was a much better salesperson. Soon, Sarah had orders coming in from every corner of the United States. In 1910, she opened the Madam C. J. Walker Manufacturing Company. A few tears of joy escaped her eyes. The jingling of the keys opening the doors of her own building was one of the best sounds she had ever heard.

After many years of hard work, Sarah decided it was time to retire. She built a big house outside of New York City and spent her time tending the garden. Lelia took over travelling and selling Madam C. J. Walker's products in her place.

Sarah had built an empire. She had shown countless women how to care for their hair, and countless more how to make money for themselves. Today, she is known as America's first self-made millionaire.

MORE FROM REBEL GIRLS!

Let stories about real-life women and girls entertain and inspire you.

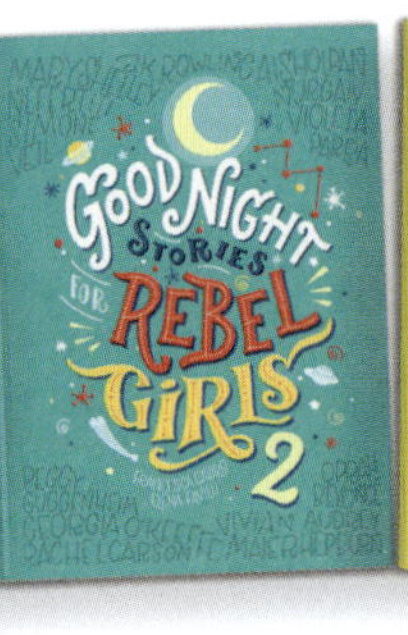

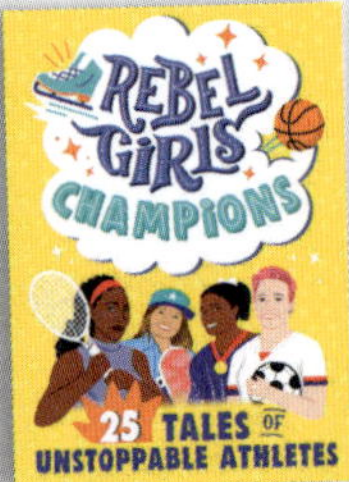

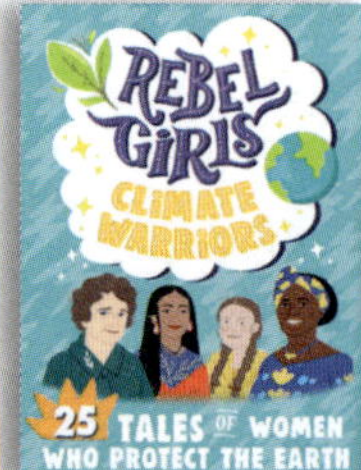

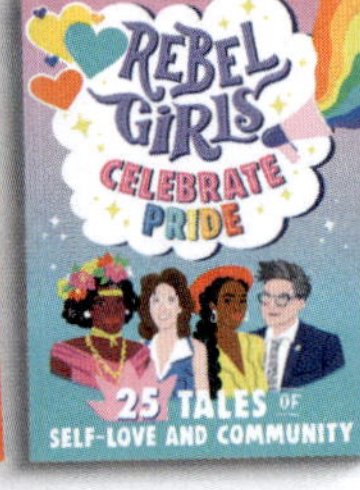

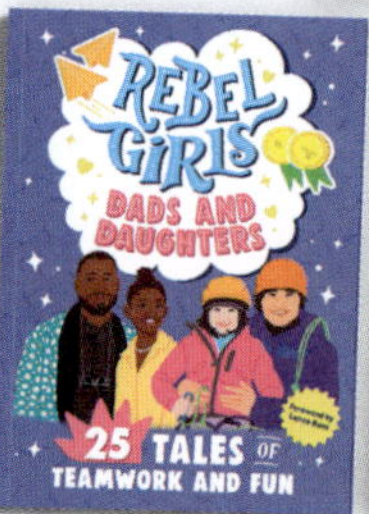

Enjoy interactive books and gifts!

The *Growing Up Powerful* series is filled with helpful advice and Q&As between tweens and experts.

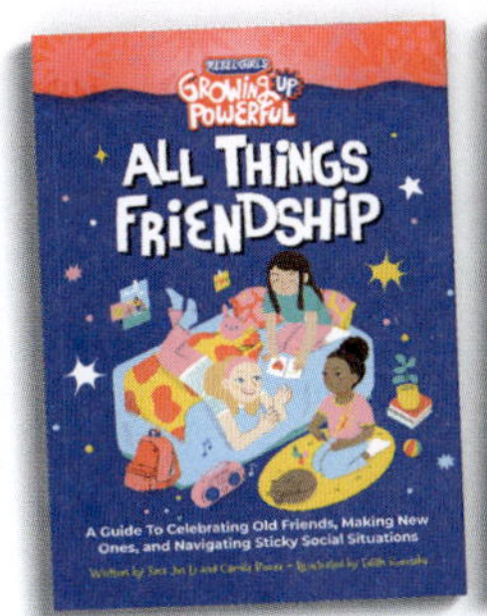

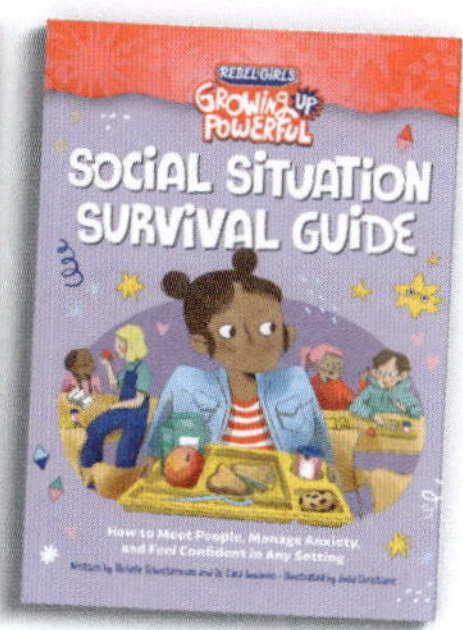

Read letters, poems, essays, and more from 145 extraordinary teens and women.

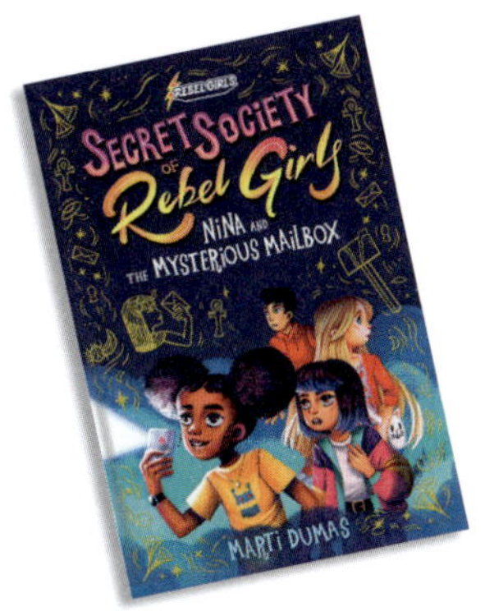

Go on an incredible middle-grade adventure with *Nina and the Mysterious Mailbox.*

PLUS! LISTEN TO REBEL GIRLS STORIES

Scan to hear exciting stories about extraordinary women and girls from all around the world and throughout history.

ABOUT REBEL GiRLS

REBEL GiRLS, a certified B Corporation, is a global, multi-platform empowerment brand dedicated to helping raise the most inspired and confident generation of girls. The brand purposefully creates content, products, and experiences to empower Generation Alpha girls and equip them with the knowledge and tools they need to thrive. Because confident girls will radically transform the world.

With a growing community of 36 million self-identified Rebel Girls spanning more than 115 countries, the brand engages with Gen Alpha through its book series, premier app, events, and merchandise. To date, Rebel Girls has sold more than 11 million books in 62 languages and reached 65 million digital listens/views. Award recognition includes the *New York Times* bestseller list, 2022 Apple Design Award for Social Impact, 10 Webby Awards, and more.

As a B Corp, we're part of a global community of businesses that meet high standards of social and environmental impact.

JOiN THE REBEL GiRLS COMMUNiTY!

Visit rebelgirls.com and join our email list for exclusive sneak peeks, promos, activities, and more. You can also email us at hello@rebelgirls.com.

- YouTube: youtube.com/rebelgirls
- App: rebelgirls.com/audio
- Podcast: rebelgirls.com/podcast
- Facebook: facebook.com/rebelgirls
- Instagram: @rebelgirls
- Email: hello@rebelgirls.com
- Web: rebelgirls.com

If you liked this book, please take a moment to review it wherever you prefer!